DRESS REHEARSALS

DRESS REHEARSALS

Madison Godfrey

First published in 2023

Joan, an imprint of
Allen & Unwin
Cammeraygal Country
83 Alexander Street
Crows Nest NSW 2065
Australia
Phone: (61 2) 8425 0100
Email: info@allenandunwin.com
Web: www.allenandunwin.com

Allen & Unwin acknowledges the Traditional Owners of the Country on which we live and work. We pay our respects to all Aboriginal and Torres Strait Islander Elders, past and present.

A catalogue record for this book is available from the National Library of Australia

ISBN 978 1 76106 857 7

Set in 11.5/18 pt Bembo by Bookhouse
Printed and bound in Australia by Pegasus Media & Logistics

10 9 8 7 6 5 4 3 2

The paper in this book is FSC® certified.
FSC® promotes environmentally responsible, socially beneficial and economically viable management of the world's forests.

For all those beside me in the mosh pits of gender

‘And I watch you, your reversal,
it’s an honest thing when there’s no one there.
Some days they feel like dress rehearsals,
some days I watch and you don’t care.’

—La Dispute

CONTENTS

PART ONE

PART TWO

THE FEMME FATALE GOES HOME

PART THREE

This book references sexual violence, murder, eating disorders, gender dysphoria and menstruation. Please read these poems in a way that is safe for you.

PART ONE

'There is something else at work than just nostalgia, though, and that is the disparity between me and the girl these memories happened to.'

—Tavi Gevinson

WHEN I GROW UP I WANT TO BE THE MERCH GIRL

Sighing like a swimsuit model who got fired yesterday. Boyfriend's band shirt tied on one side. Silver belly ring aligning with the trestle table. Glaring at her Nokia. Permanent-marker forearms. Later, the merch girl leans over my sister sink in the graffitied bathroom. Smudges her eyeliner with precision. Undoes her middle part like a top button. I don't know if she goes to school or plays an instrument, but I've seen her fit a man's entire tongue in her mouth without flinching. I want to advertise Gildan shirts and burnt CDs. I want to look grown-up enough to trust with a metal box. Want to angle my hips like armrests. Want my shoulders mapped by the longitude of lacy straps. She's always adjusting a bejewelled handbag, while my backpack bulges with a water bottle and a glad-wrapped snack. When I grow up I want a man to ask me to sit behind his pride, while he sings about my thighs to a room of girls with black gauze turning their legs into ladders. Blinks with only one of his eyes.

IMPULSE

Months later, I am still thinking about the two teen girls who saw me and knew I wouldn't tell. Everyone else in the supermarket was their mother. Every other mouth had a muscle-memory snarl. Two girls huddled together like baby geese that ran away the same season they learnt the softness of feathers. Whispering. Selecting. Spraying. Artificial flowers bloomed like factory fumes. Rotating. Sniffing. Too grown for giggling. Draped over spaghetti shoulders, the fragrance smelt like a sarcastic *sorry*. Maybe they used half the tin. Maybe I shouldn't have smiled. Standing in the same aisle, I felt precisely halfway between the girl with cigarette sleeves and the mother who grips the hoodie.

UNIFORM

'Most mornings you see the face of a boy in the mirror. You expect to fall in love with him.'

—Mary Jean Chan

The bricks my father laid in his primary school days visible from our letterbox. Still, I wasn't trusted to carry the girl of my body across two suburban streets. She was heavy and shadowed like a cloud about to burst. She was an adult-sized backpack that engulfed my child-sized wingspan. If dictionaries define uniform as 'something that remains the same in all cases and at all times, unchanging in form or character', what is the word for an outfit applied differently to different children? My blue pleated skirt: an aspirational short. The first time I complained, it was because I wanted to play soccer on the school oval. I concealed: made my reasons more feminine, more pastel, more likely to be heard from a watermelon Lip Smacker mouth. Claimed I wanted to cartwheel. A decade since, my body has never achieved such inversion. Mostly, I wanted to thud like the boys who pushed their scuffed knees against the doorways of classrooms. I wanted to wear dirt like a personality trait / like a tough badge / like the way gravel gets in your palms but doesn't stay inside after the skin has healed. I didn't want to be a boy, I just wanted to try boyhood on, to eat lunch with my legs bent and spread, my crotch a glorious landscape of grey material, a body allowed to walk itself to school.

HARRY STYLES IS INTERVIEWED ON A BEACH AND THE HORIZON ALIGNS WITH HIS SIGHS

I have never been brave enough to wear white pants. My mouth is melodramatic on the best days. Has a habit of spilling whatever I am trying to keep inside. Yet, Harry manages both aesthetics and emotions. Splits his secrets into segments like ripe mandarins. Their juice does not spit. Their pips do not shoot. Even fruit obeys his wishes. He wears pristine pants beside the beach. Speaks about his upbringing. Ponders whether this confidence is something he wanted, or something he inherited without asking. Says, *my gut is the only thing I do trust.* In the comments section, strangers categorise this content as free counselling. Praise his magnetism. Construct commandments from body language. Even Harry has gone to therapy. He toes a tightrope of humility, balancing between fantasy and possibility. Sonic waves synchronise with his breath. Unshaven enough that you can imagine him visiting a supermarket, grasping a tomato, squeezing for ripeness, feeling it slip from his grasp. Then flinching as it falls to the shoe-scuffed floor and rolls towards a stranger. She retrieves it, smiles at a fandom's favourite face, yet does not recognise him. I imagine Harry accepting the tomato. I wonder if he'd place it back on the pile, or if he'd take his mistakes home and make a meal of them. Maybe wear white pants while he ate.

In the interview, Harry rolls his eyes towards a colour-corrected horizon. Somewhere: a piano is perfectly in tune, someone tries on a shoe that fits just right, a car approaches an empty country road. Maybe Harry owns multiple pairs of white pants. Swaps out the stained ones. Convinces us that we can be immaculate, too.

I GREW UP A SHADOW GIRL, WITH A MAN OUTLINED INSIDE ME

When I was fifteen in a toilet cubicle next to Tabitha,
I exclaimed *IT'S HERE* with my school skirt skimming
my ankles, white socks with two blue stripes, disinfectant
dispensers hanging beside blu-tacked announcements.

When I was fifteen, sweating through my palms, standing
in a carpeted counselling office. The man with rectangular
eyes repeated, *show her what you did to yourself*
until blood was no longer a milestone but a symptom.

When I was fifteen and wanted so badly to be anything
but *girl.* To be blood itself, not the cotton that catches it.
Wanted to be the softness of a football mid-air, when
it exists between release and recipient (untouched).

I couldn't play sports in a skirt. I couldn't play truant
with this body. My unshrinkable shame formed a photo
frame: positioned me precisely within the shadow
of some woman I could have / should have been.

I couldn't play sports in a skirt. So I never learnt to sprint.
Instead I spent a decade dodging labels and assigning genders
like 'tomboy' when I truly meant 'almost boy'. Tabitha taught me
how to handle the bleeding, but I hadn't addressed the wound.

LIKE A TOUCH LAMP COVERED IN DUST

I mourn the missing memory. What was pleasure before I knew the word for it? When did I learn that an orgasm could grow with the curvature of my toes? When someone asks about the first time, I never speak of tongue, never of tap, never of speed hump. Still, I do not remember the first time that my bare crotch could do more than make a baby, or make a boy love me back. My arousal: a gift I was not allowed to unwrap.

SIXTEEN

I stuff lyrics in my skirt pockets like tissues in a bra. I have a crush on a boy who makes me feel small when he stares at me. I look down and blush on cue. Yet when I stand in front of a kickdrum each foot/pedal/collision carves me a new heartbeat. My sternum thrums like a tuning fork. This is the only room where I am allowed to yell. Elsewhere, my quiet is a currency I am trading for almost-affections.   We lie on the carpet of his family living room. Near a shelf of DVD spines, beside a couch instead of on it. *Call of Duty* paused on the television. He presses play on 'Such Small Hands' and I love it, immediately. An obsession I begin to define myself by, after a year of pouring myself into the tiny holes of his belt, pretending to be a useful puncture.   If mimicry was a love language I had not yet learnt, would I have adopted this song the same way?   Sitting on the edge of his bed, facing a wall of band posters pulled from the centre of magazines, he asks, *who do you love more, me or La Dispute?* All the glossy men who borrow one another's black jeans glare like stern fathers. My answer is the only time I ever break a pinky promise on purpose.   Even at sixteen, I knew I could never love a boy like I love a band. There are no epiphanies in bedroom eyes. My body, still far too much my body, when he held me. My heart had no religion when it raced for him.   I am still searching for some of the songs he showed me, but I have mostly stopped seeing him in empty supermarket aisles.

THE NECK BECAME A BRUISE LIKE THE GIRL BECAME A WOMAN

suddenly and without permission / on top of a washing machine in a locked laundry / truth or dare in the swimming pool before pick-up / in the backseat before the clumsy drug deal / accidentally during lovemaking / purposefully during fucking / once I wore a bruise like an engraved collar / once I administered a hickey like a flag stabbed into land / when my mother saw his neck she laughed the whole way home / the drive took three hours / the drive took an entire adolescence / the drive folded my rebellion into a love note / following the very first time, my father compared me to property / Mum giggled in the doorway / how lucky we would be to own our homes, even temporarily / when I said bruise, I meant a betrayal trapped beneath skin / how girlhood went to the party wanting to be overtly known / returned as a landlord / a cartographer of owned places / too drunk to drive her desire home.

THE ONLY LEOPARD PRINT I HAVE EVER OWNED STILL HANGS IN MY CHILDHOOD BEDROOM

This was the type of party you go shopping for. The dress needed to speak. A pleather boob-tube bodice sewn to a leopard-print skirt. Skin stained by first love, but I sat on Jeremy's lap instead. Still glanced for *him* around the side of the house where kids gurgled into Gatorade bottles. I looked too grown-up for *just* Jeremy. It was the type of party where everyone was pretending to be loved.

I search for a photo online but cannot remember his last name.

Jeremy—

Jeremy—

Jeremy—

His profile picture is an ultrasound.

Madison—

Madeleine—

Magdalene—

I interrogate all the lives I could've lived by now. How many men I could've made into absent fathers. How many widows I could've made from my own ambition. On Monday, Jeremy had tonsillitis too. That was the last time I wore leopard print, and yet the dress remains; a reminder of the life I almost wore   myself down for.

LEOPARD PRINT: EPILOGUE

In the photographs we look so much younger than we do in the memories. The well I wanted to pour my ambition into was simply a boy doing bongs in the backyard. Still, we liked the same sad albums. We shared earphones on the bus. He handwrote me paragraphs of lyrics. Our side fringes like mirror images. The undeserving boy I once loved is now an undeserving man, yet the girl of me continues missing him.

SONNET FOR LONGING

After Sam Rush

fan girl / fan girl / fan girl / fan girl / fan girl
fan girl / fan girl / fan girl / fan girl / fan girl
fan girl / fan girl / fight girl / fan girl / fan girl
fan girl / fan girl / freeze girl / fan girl / fan girl
fan girl / fan girl / flight girl / fan girl / fan girl
fan girl / fan girl / fawn girl / fan girl / fan girl
fan girl / blog girl / queue girl / wail girl / wait girl
fan girl / fan girl / bad girl / mad girl / sad girl
fan girl / front man / band man / bad man / his girl
fan mouth / fan chest / fan lips / fan breast / young girl
how young? / yes, girl / you, girl / good girl / shush girl
yell girls / ache girls / sob girls / loud girls / these girls
us girls / fan girls / for girls / my girls / still, girls
fan girls / fan girls / fan girls / fan girls / fan girls

MERCH GIRL: THE FIRST TIME

She protected the stock while he protected his image. How expensive would it be, to explain the truth of the teenage girl in his passenger seat? Unless she was useful: an enthusiastic employee, earning an apprenticeship in monetising longing. He sold more shirts when he was single. If her youth was stored behind the moat of a trestle table, no customers could reach out and hold it up to the light, saying *something about this, doesn't feel quite right.*

GIRLHOOD AS JOKE: DRIVEWAY / DAUGHTER

hey dude, chill out   we're all just here to have fun   I didn't mean anything by it   *What's the difference between my driveway and my daughter?*   don't be such a killjoy   you're overreacting   *I pull out of my driveway.*   I have a hot girlfriend / female friends / a sister / a mother / a co-worker /   she doesn't hate me, so obviously I'm not one of *those*   can't you take a joke? you're the problem   all those bands torn apart by lies   obviously I haven't fucked my daughter   and if I did, she would've liked it   *Laughs*   nah, just joking, I don't have a daughter / but I still get called 'Daddy'   *Laughs*   if you make a big deal out of this we'll give you a reason to be scared / they'll recognise your face / we protect our own   we love our female fans / they look so good at the gigs / they mosh with the guys   our shirts are unisex so their tits never quite fit   nobody gets groped / they'd tell us if they got groped   nobody's ever told us / nobody's ever told on us   nah you obviously don't understand   *Laughs*   I can feel you choking and I blame your throat   what's stuck up your cunt? / bit grumpy today? / heavy flow?   it was your fault   we just wanted to cheer you up   why are you blaming us?   it's so much easier to blame yourself.

GIRLHOOD AS JOKE: CYCLE

You're an adult dressed   like a teenage dream
        when he spits that joke into a microphone.
Back when you measured my hem with your hands,
        your bandmates called you   *babysitter.*

He spits into a microphone,
        positions girls as punchlines.
Your bandmates call you   *babysitter*
                                        a decade later.

Girls positioned as punchlines
        in a room of speakers   where nobody speaks up.
A decade later,
            do you remember how small I looked,   lying on stage?

A room of speakers where nobody speaks up,
        gives a man a microphone and chuckles at misogyny.
Do you remember how small I looked,   lying on stage?
        Telling myself I was old enough.

Give a man a microphone and chuckle at misogyny.
You were there,
        telling yourself I was old enough.
Does the new girlfriend know how you muffled me?

You were there.
    I was flinching.
        Does the new girlfriend know how you muffled me?
            Like a retainer that barely fit in my mouth.

Flinching. I was wearing
            eighteen
like a retainer that barely fit in my mouth,
like a band shirt I squeezed my entire identity inside.

I was eighteen
        when you measured my worth with your hands.
Like a band shirt, I squeezed my entire identity inside
                adults dressed like teenage dreams.

GIRLHOOD AS JOKE: PUNCHLINE

Misogyny takes centre stage and nobody walks out, not even her.

NO MORE THIN LINE DRAWINGS OF WOMANHOOD

Not an elegant advert.
Not an expensive fineliner.
Not a calligraphy course.
Not a momentary sweep.
Not a curated accident.
Not a tattoo taken from a tampon wrapper.
Not a grieving snail trail.
Not a body defined by boundaries.
Not an annotated margin.
Not a hip that doesn't click.
Not a silhouette too slender for texture.
Not an unsmudged stencil.
Not a curving one-way road.
Not a bridge between absences.
I want to be the opposite of a shadow,
want to look like all the places
light touches and stays.
I am not a thin
line, a perfectly placed axis.
This will take longer than a bathroom break.

They were a pair of brown 'short shorts' that I called my 'Lara Croft shorts'. Borrowed my father's belt for a makeshift holster. In my favourite scene, Lara suspends her body between two bungee elastics, like a spider with sex appeal. She wraps her legs around a chandelier and punches an invader in the face. Her knuckles never bruise. When she spin-kicks, she points her toes. Online, I watch videos titled 'Training for Tomb Raider' and 'Becoming Lara' to learn what an initiation into this elegant violence would look like. It is multidisciplinary: a wrestling ring shaped like a jewellery box, how to grasp a weapon like a lover, a gymnastic braid stretching down between her shoulder blades, a bead of sweat that never leaves her brow. Both actors who have become Lara describe the sharp angles of her strength, a new character chiselled from their own physiques. They are set-piece chandeliers; delicate enough to decorate a room, but strong enough to support a woman's weight. Becoming Lara means becoming so desirable that it's dangerous. The burden of being wanted, another strain on the structure that suspends you.

BECOMING LARA: ADDENDUM

The year before I was born, Toby Gard designed a bad-ass brunette named Laura Cruz. Later whitewashed to Croft: a glamorisation of colonisation. Her torso visibly taut despite pixellation. Her shorts still short shorts. Garters emphasised her upper thighs. Chest engorged by an unfixed glitch. Greasy adolescent thumbs directed all her movements. Her figure obeyed. Pressing certain combos made her breasts bounce when she lunged forward. Even my adolescent rebellion was directed by the male gaze. My aspirations, man-made. Even my dad desired Lara.

DICHOTOMY

Your closet is a case study in belonging. Shove aside your ironed collars for the shirt you saved for today. Colour-coordinate your socks and your scarf. You marked your calendar the morning you scored tickets. Meet with your friends early, to stretch the anticipation over a few more hours, until it becomes thin and wet like spit at the dinner table during grace. Paint flushed cheeks with your favourite colours. Use your fingers because tactility is tender: a boundary line between animalistic and intimate. On the train in, sing the song you love most, the one you're excited to hear later, with a carriage of throats who have collected the same drink coasters and posters as you. March like a procession. Edge affection with aggression. Arrive at the show and squirm in your seat. Turn around and gossip about your faves to the audience members behind you. You're betting on the young brunette with legs that drive a bargain. This guy's here for the captain, the straight shooter, the family man he secretly longs to be. Nobody questions the absurdity of a grass ocean located in the centre of a city. When it's over, you'll rush to the barrier and push your palm forward, hoping to share the sweat of a man who just kicked your attention around a field for hours. As you leave, a crowd of teenagers are erecting tents in a line outside the arena, writing numbers on their hands like temporary jerseys. You mock them for melodrama, as if the glitter above their eyes does not contain tiny mirrors.

GOOD GUYS IS AN APPLIANCE STORE

Mid-conversation, my uncle whispers a catcall across the passenger seat, as if I have not walked down this same street. His steering wheel does not flinch. All the good men I know have been bad men to someone else.

My partner gets too drunk and treats consent like a suggestion. Arriving home, we find his bed is the same size. I wait all night, but no shadows haunt him in a staring contest. I listen to him breathe while I clutch my car keys. All good men were bad men once.

A memory dressed like an old friend enters my favourite café. The sunlight doesn't avoid his skin. My favourite barista smiles at him. Nobody clambers onto their table in protest. He pays with a card but the bank does not decline, assertive alarms don't interrupt slow and snazzy jazz, his sesame bagel is not burnt.

After the night it happened, I salvaged the secret from the bin. Wrapped it inside a makeup wipe. Kept the evidence for an entire month, before disposing of it. Determined that nobody would know that this good man, the one who made me breakfast in the morning, was still a bad man who had not learnt better.

CHILD OF THE HURRICANE

Like Dorothy but less glamorous. Slippers are fluffy rather than sparkling. Toto is a rescue cat with ringworm. The kitchen tap drips all night and I name this a natural disaster. How else could I explain what it is like to stay awake for days and never overturn the pillow? Everyone I adore is a main character who chases their insecurities past brick roads where brickies mostly catcall the conventional girls. I know this because I have walked behind, witnessed from a distance, like a large coat that never touches skin. Nobody told the scarecrow to smile. After I shaved my head, the wind picked up, and it carried me elsewhere. When I disavowed womanhood, my shortest skirts burnt at the stake. When I reclaimed pigtails, my hemlines grew teeth. I learnt how to exist in public without treating myself like public property. During those weeks when I did not leave Kansas, or my apartment, nobody placed an unbeaten heart on my doorstep. Dorothy wanted to go home, but I wanted to become one. Us queers with our short hair, our charity shops, our resilience. I hold hands with all my friends. I hold hands with all my lovers too. There's no place like here, right here. We give human names to hurricanes because they are capable of change. I am growing and this is a good thing. Even if you granted me one wish, I would not want to wake up elsewhere. When Dorothy says she is never going to leave *here* again, I hope she means *herself*.

POSTER GIRL

I was the good girl at my private school. Pleated skirt and memorised Catholicism. Teacher's pet with a stray crush on a bad boy, but even he couldn't lead me astray. Awards at assemblies. Recited verses at church. Waited for love to undo my blazer. One piercing, through my belly button, that my mother allowed at sixteen: a rebellion so small that I asked for permission first. I was not depressed enough to hurt others. Graduated second in my class. Not quite perfect but nothing to be concerned about. I remember students joking before exams. Saying, *fuck this I'll just become a stripper.* That was a comic we found online. All of us good girls, clutching pristine futures like porcelain we could not afford. Mr Matheson walked me out of graduation, elbow in elbow, a procession to greatness. Two years later my charisma was chain-smoking on a strip club staircase. Using equations I had studied diligently, I counted my dollars quickly. All the bad girls from high school are mothers now.

MOST PEOPLE I KNOW HAVE HAD SEX WHILE LISTENING TO THE ARCTIC MONKEYS

'I couldn't get the boy to kill me, but I wore his jacket for the longest time.'

—Richard Siken

Intro.

The man in black jeans slicks back his hair and gyrates.
Women scream as if there is an emergency occurring
south of their throats, and panic is trying to clamber out.

Verse.

Around Walyalup's bonfire, a stranger in a denim jacket pushes
me out of his way and I fall in lust immediately. I try to catch
his cigarette ash with my fingertips. When we kiss his lips are loud
with someone else's shape. I do not ask for more. I do not need to.
To be almost a woman, undesired but touched: this is enough.

Bridge.

At sixteen I went to concerts with my stockings laddered. Longed
for someone to climb up them, like Rapunzel with less romance.

Chorus.

Harry Styles sells out a concert in my hometown.
That night, the strip clubs are louder than usual.
If our wives can have their fantasies,
why can't we?

Verse.

When I masturbate, I picture a man I have never met thrusting himself between all my bad decisions. His hair is scruffy like an actor's after a sex scene. His biceps hold me in place, I am an instrument he did not pay for. Someone else's lipstick is smeared across his nipples.

Pre-Chorus.

If you listen closely to any Arctic Monkeys album, you can hear
the thrust of a groin against an instrument.

Chorus.

In lucid dreams, you cannot look in mirrors. When I touch
myself, I am never the body, only the sensation forming
beneath someone else's hands. Even alone, I kneel open
mouthed at the foot of my own bed and apologise for gasping.

Interlude.

Women are not allowed to be sexual unless they learn the rules first:
this is when you scream / this is when you dance /
you can only desire me because I do not want you / clutch
your menthol cigarette / lace up your boots / tighter /
take off your underwear under the table / wait here /

Outro.

In crowded mosh pits, shuddering might be dancing. If I lie
very still during sex, I can convince myself
I am only an instrument, that he mistook my body
for something of higher value. That he was saving me
rather than teaching me how to stay quiet.

Applause.

CRUSH

Text them. Having a crush is powerful. Think about the word. Not wither, not want. It's crumpling a piece of paper in your palm. Proving that you have the capacity to care without the ownership of *relationship.* Forgetting is a skill reserved for those with warmer hands. When your crush slept in your bed for the first time, there was a summer solstice beneath your sheets. You realised that people who are in love do not use multiple blankets. Once, when you named someone *crush*, they recoiled. Do not define yourself by their distance. Feeling with full force might be a burden, but it keeps your shoulders strong. Text the person you *like-like*. Joke with your favourite barista. Marry your suburb. Propose to the softest parts of yourself. Ask them to stay. Promise you'll stay.

Silence In Three Parts

SILENCE: PART ONE

Setting: the shared bathroom of a suburban home

My mother raised me
in a quiet house, that
resembled her mouth.

She left the box in our bathroom,
a piece of paper providing
instructions, not experience.

I found it waiting for me. First love
had made my blood rush so much
that it escaped from unexpected places.

I grew up without Google,
so my search engine was
a mirror, positioned

awkwardly upon the bathroom
tiles. I was so pink. I wanted to ask
my lover's tongue how it navigated

all these absences. I didn't know
how to ask. I didn't know how
to insert something other than him

into me. The instructions were
written in adult language. I learnt
to masturbate for moisture. It hurt

less if I thought of him first. It hurt
more if I was rushed. Becoming a
woman was a hasty event which

happened mostly on bathroom floors.
In rooms that echoed with voices of other
women, how they contorted themselves

into these same silences.

SILENCE: PART TWO

Setting: changing room

My mother didn't know where I was earning my money.
Didn't ask why I returned home at 6am with a duffel bag
heavy with stilettos. The sound they made against each other
was unmistakable to anyone who wasn't desperate to ignore it.

Most girls wore tampons. Some used sponges but that scared me.
I imagined the kitchen sponge, smooth yellow
scratchy green,
jammed deep inside of me.

Just cut the string.

In the changing room, I watched a dancer mount
a wall with one leg, so she was wide open
for the nurse to inspect. This nurse wore red
fishnets and a matching garter belt.

Scissors in one hand, cocktail in the other.
She inspected the patient. Placed her glass on the edge
of a sink. Pried open folds as though they were pages
of a novel she had already read.

Snip.

The patient dismounted, grabbed the nurse's cocktail, sculled it. Tucked a finger inside of herself and pushed upwards.

Let's go.

SILENCE: PART THREE

Setting: the same suburban bathroom, four years later

My legs are parted like a disjointed spider.
The tiny mirror, once used to discover myself,
is now held in desperation. I have fit four fingers
inside my vagina, more than ever before.

My mother once told me you cannot lose a tampon inside yourself.

I spit on my hand, rub my clit like a prayer book and
convince myself that I am not crying. Nobody told me
that vaginas are deep caves with tight corners. Nobody
provided a diagram that documents this panic.

I wonder if Medicare will cover this.

My thumb joins the party. Picturing the fisting pornography
I once recoiled in front of, I assume this is physically
possible. I lean my head back, elongate my vertebrae. I imagine
a chiselled abdomen mid-thrust, large hands with calloused
palms, a cigarette being sucked in slow motion.

Nothing is wrong. Nothing is lost inside of me.
Nothing is wrong. Nothing is lost inside of me.

Nothing is wrong. Nothing is lost—
I gasp when I grasp it.

The tampon is the colour of red lipstick the morning after,
once the original shade has smudged upon so many other
mouths. I hold it like a newborn and promise to stop
cutting strings. To never again shove my shame so deep
inside my body, that I cannot salvage it the next morning.

MIDNIGHT SNEAKERS

You never wear heels when you go out drinking. Walk alone past the park with the lake that has been drained multiple times for bodies of women who newspapers didn't notice. Nobody wants to speak about this at Sunday picnics. A passing car opens its mouth. Your neck crunches like a fist. Womanhood shouldn't be synonymous with survival. Everyone who loves you tells you not to walk home alone, to stop wearing headphones, to treat your quiet nights like a grief you are inviting into their lives. You tell them that women are being murdered for much less than this.

I MISGENDER MYSELF IN THE MEMORIES

'I'm not a woman, but part of me / is always going to be a teenage girl.'

—Lyd Havens

Here, in the black box of my nostalgia, the walls are papered with gig posters from decades that survived other decades to become themselves. Scrape off enough layers, and you'll find receipts of the shapes I made myself into, squeezing adolescence into adulthood. Beware the blu-tack soaked in blood. Round the corner, the concrete is stained by handbag goon bags that burst like a belly belted too tight around the waist. In the bin, another pair of black stockings I sacrificed to the mosh pit, for the temporary sensation of getting hit instead of getting hit *on*. Over there is the water fountain where I bent over and bled like a loose tap in the night. My first blood nose: a souvenir of a spin kick from a boot that did not stop to see what it collided with. I was always a collision in slow motion. I was always a girl, even though I was never a girl. But how else could I explain what the mouth was trying to become? Not a mouth itself, but an orifice; an absence I could parade in public. I grew up between a knee-high barrier and a chain-link fence made from men in black band hoodies. My parents warned that if I kept coming home with those bruises, my thighs would tell the same stories forever. It wasn't the bruises that stayed. Ten years later, if you put me in that same room, with those same people, I would elbow to the front and shout until someone shoved a microphone between my teeth. I wouldn't remember that I had a body. I wouldn't care that I had grown tall enough to see the look in his eyes. Still, I am the mouth in those photographs. Still, I am bleeding while a man's boot keeps spinning. Still, I am putting the girl in fangirl. Once, in the graffitied bathroom, I sobbed on the floor while the world was ending. A man told me it wasn't. But in the first moment that your skin stops belonging to you and becomes a picnic blanket pressed into damp grass, doesn't the world end, a little bit? The venue owner pulled me to my feet, led me to a secret door, and welcomed me back. The men on stage, the men who put their arms around me at house parties, the men who bought me a diet coke at Subway, the men who were all old enough to drive me home, were playing a song that I knew.

SPIDERS ON MY LASH LINE

I wear fake eyelashes to the punk gig. My friend sits between my legs, applying the mask of a muse onto what was once my face. I want to visit hyper-femininity like a city built by men, who mapped the streetlamps but never pole danced on them. It has been twelve years since anyone glued extra lashes to my own. I was a choreographed child doing a bend-back in ruby spandex. Now the leotard is spray-on skin I wear beneath my clothing. Still performing for the back row, which is to say, still looking through the crowd for a man who does not yet love me back. The woman on stage screams, *I don't wanna talk about basic human rights* and I whisper the words like a sermon. Rage is a religion, something I practise in private, kneel beside my bed like a promising young woman. I want a prophet who is pretty *and* powerful. I want to wear lip gloss to the protest. I want to gouge out a rapist's eyes with a fresh manicure.

PART TWO

THE FEMME FATALE GOES HOME

'Where she appears, gender trouble is inevitable.'

—Christina Grübler

THE FEMME FATALE APPEARS

First, I walk in on the femme fatale in the bathtub, bent over like a freeze frame of a myth. It is Sunday, the day of scrubbing and wiping every surface until I can sleep soundly. I walk into the bathroom and it feels as if a heat lamp has been left on. A substance, somewhere between mist and smoke, coats each cabinet handle. She has filled the space with something unworldly, something unspeakable, something soaked and aching and entirely hers. The room responds to her presence like a lava lamp to touch. One of her legs is bent, foot raised, her toes grip the porcelain lip. Her body folded in half, an angle so awkward it could only exist in a fashion magazine. Her body resembles a body in a fogged-up mirror. Her edges blur even after I blink, then blink again. Living alone has taught me to fear footsteps but she is more apparition than intruder. She sighs as though she knows I am listening. Pastel razor held like a baton, contorting to make herself smooth. I close the bathroom door behind me, wipe the handle, blame the bleach.

THE FEMME FATALE UNDRESSES

I catch the femme fatale pouring micellar water over her face as if mascara were original sin. I am waddling to the toilet at 2am. She is bent over my bathroom sink, with grey marle granny panties hoisted high enough to hold her belly (without holding it in). I keep micellar water behind the mirror because it's the gentlest way to remove an evening. Excess liquid hits her shoulders the same way waterfalls are described in romance novels. She doesn't flinch at the spill that will surely follow, but the mess never reaches a surface. The tiles glint. The sink grins dryly. Everything evaporates around her, as if air itself is trying to impress. I imagine her walking through a storm without an umbrella while her perm persists, existing in its own ecosystem. Tonight, as she stretches over the basin, there is a warmth emanating from her bareness that is the opposite of sweat or sex. Rather, the lover's calves that you press cold feet against under the covers. Or, a laundry hamper where a cat just slept. As she wipes her face with the flannel my grandmother made, I watch her pimples remember their anger, her brows sigh then sparsen, her eyelashes kick off their heavy edges. The basin glows opalescent pink beneath her presence, as though even porcelain is bashful to see her undress in this ordinary way. With the slow precision of a human statue, her arm extends towards me, one pearl earring posed upon her open palm. As I grasp it, she smiles and extinguishes the light. I sit on the toilet in complete darkness, a pearl earring poking through the top pocket of my pyjamas.

THE FEMME FATALE BREAKS A NAIL

I come home from work and she is doing the dishes that I left beside the sink last night. Dark red polish has started to separate from her submerged nails. I gasp and tell her to stop. Tell her to preserve what draws attention to her extremities. Tell her it's not worth the sacrifice, to dull your public self for private neatness. She throws her head back as if laughing, but no sound escapes her open mouth. She adorns rubber gloves, but the moment they're on, she reaches to her elbow and grasps the plastic edge. Peels it down her forearm with a performance worthy of silk. Then she pulls each individual finger like a masseuse clicking joints. Each edge knows flourish. Her chin raised so high she can likely see the envelopes I forgot on top of the fridge. It takes me a beat to recognise this routine. How a burlesque glove is not just a glove, but an invitation for an audience's attention to hyper-focus. Not just hoping to be looked at, but asking to be zoomed in upon. Here, she is inviting me to stare at her, all plastic glove and imperfection. Domestic bodies still have muscle memories. She pulls the plug, spits into the draining sink; a movement so quick I question my gaze.

THE FEMME FATALE LINGERS

Her body is a memory that the couch cushion keeps safe. Her bloody pads wrapped in toilet paper on the windowsill. I trip over her stilettos. I beckon her fingerprints away from all my mirrors. I ban her pout from my wine glass. I pray and her scent fits between my palms. Even when I don't see her for months, she stays like the smoke of a candle extinguished only moments before you entered a room.

THE FEMME FATALE SLEEPS OVER

I enter the bedroom freshly towelled. She is waiting, wearing a silk nightie the shade of a cloud that has never held a storm. With legs concealed under covers, even her hinted indents have elegance. She gestures to another nightie, folded on my side of the bed, and I pull it on. She looks at me as if I am just about to do something important. She pats the space beside her. The sheets are already warm. Lying on our backs, the static of silk strings electricity wires between our bodies. I worry that my breathing is too boisterous. I syncopate my inhalations then become self-conscious. Rush my pace. I worry she can feel the mattress move each time I blink. When I turn to apologise, a fresh tear is on her temple. It occurs to me, that I've never shared a bed this quiet with anyone I wasn't falling out of or into love with. What a pleasure it is to abandon longing. To go to sleep with the same amount of adoration that will stir beside you tomorrow.

THE FEMME FATALE ASKS LANA WHAT TO WEAR

I am humming and tying my shoelaces, while she stands in front of my wardrobe, trying on then flinging away each of my dresses. Her presence so familiar, I hardly notice as she starts harmonising with my hummed version of a Lana Del Rey song that I don't know the lyrics to. Her harmonies are high enough to make a wine glass nervous, but faultless enough to evoke nostalgia for a childhood spent in vetiver pews. When she tries on clothes, she resembles a beautiful woman on a shopping spree in a film. Her arms find the holes on her first attempt. In each outfit, she tilts her head. Pivots to assess. Arches her lower back. Then balloons her belly and holds the bulge as if it contains forty weeks of tiny futures. This is a graceful contortion. She spins and sighs. She strokes the seams and measures her worth in finger-widths. She mutters something about the way music makes men into seamstresses. Whenever she talks in my presence, her voice is a quiet beast at the back of her throat. She only speaks to mirrors or windows or birds and never addresses me directly. Today, somewhere between a hot pink dress and a cream gown, she mutters phrases like parts of a partially remembered prayer. *You disobedient body / you beautiful coffin / you bombshell bathed in rubble / you faulty tomb / you child wearing your mother's hope / you tardy hourglass / you bloated road / you dead-eyed end.* Her lyrics all wrong; still I keep humming.

THE FEMME FATALE ENTERS, HEARTBROKEN

—and asks me where her edges are. Tries to grasp her hips but her hands slip right through the flesh. I cut an apple into segments. I pour a mug of wine. I treat her like the human she is sure she is not. Once a warm apparition, now a ghost haunting herself. She lies on the ground and asks the ceiling fan, *why does my desire wear such unflattering silhouettes? Why do I yearn for the public parks of other suburbs? When I sway into a room, packs of men stare at me as though my silence could satiate their masculinities. On the street I am noticed, my body annotated. Yet whenever my imagination finds a person it can form a future from, they pat me on the back instead of cupping my nape. They say goodbye instead of goodnight. What good are free drinks if I am hungering for a home-cooked meal?*

THE FEMME FATALE HIDES HER HANDS

I wonder if Norma Jean got premenstrual pimples / I wonder if Mary daydreamed different ways to be holy forever / I wonder if I will ever be as beautiful as I could be / Will my death only be didactic if I'm wearing winged eyeliner? / Does the colour of the mouth change what it is allowed to ask? / Does desire have a scent? / Why does it make me smell like carved meat? / I want to ask the femme fatale if she would sacrifice all this attention for an early night / I want to learn her middle name / I want to know about the first time she felt sexy / And I think of the friend who told me about her wedding night / When her blindfolded groom held hands with a line of women and had to identify his wife from all those anonymous grips / I wonder if anyone has ever recognised what my extremities wanted / Or if I ever reveal myself without reaching for a zipper / Maybe the femme fatale's hands are her most private parts / Everywhere else is a canvas men have assigned nicknames to / But if she's always gripping a glass, a gun, a smoke, a hip or a hope . . . nobody can see the scar in the centre of her palm.

THE FEMME FATALE GOES HOME

How boring, to be beautiful forever. I walk in on her dancing with legs bent and posture crumpled. A mirror placed face down. *She is dangerous in her defiance. She burned the birthing books. She wore only the apron.* She moves her shoulders side to side, a knife in one hand and a lime in the other. She cups the fruit in her palm and carefully cuts, still swaying. *Does she ever get to dance without a man or his camera?* She gallops clumsy-loud towards the dining table, squeezes juice into a bourbon glass. She gulps and opens her mouth wider than I knew she could. Her burp is a prayer I feel guilty for overhearing: a confession shaped like air. *What purpose would a throat have, if not an elite room that men can enter? If a woman is a speakeasy, who decides the password?* On my living room carpet, she drags her bare feet and sips her drink and squints her eyes and slumps her shoulders and disobeys basslines and unclenches expectations and wiggles her butt and spills her drink and flings her head back and remembers her mouth and still, and still, no siren song comes out.

THE FEMME FATALE SLURS HER DESIRES

She comes home slurring up a story of a man with tattoos everywhere but his stomach. Says that even the most intimidating observers still cultivate a spot so soft that only their lovers share the secret. She slopes against a frame. Demands a story. Asks, *where is your soft spot?* And I think of the double crown on my scalp, how at birth I was more vulnerable to blunt force but also *twice the princess.* She says no, it must be a landscape that nobody has included in a guidebook. My scalp too owned. My scars in poems. I ask what parts of her are still private. She stumbles then topples a secret: describes the freckle between her thighs. A spot that holds the attention of tongues not eyes. How lovers are either too focused or too distracted to notice such a small stain. I don't need to ask for specifics. The same sun has snuck beneath my waistband. I have seen this souvenir in a handheld mirror. Suddenly, we are the same, except for how we wear the shame. She slings it over her shoulder. I shove it down, into my fist, into my pocket.

THE FEMME FATALE RETURNS WITH CUM IN HER HAIR

She points to her undercut and giggles. I grimace then fill a bathtub and sit behind her, tugging a tortoiseshell comb. The substance looks like a spider web from a haunted house at an amusement park. Something you might fear if left alone in the dark. As I switch between comb and conditioner, she tells me of the man and the width of his hands. Tells me how it feels to gift someone permission to look directly into you. How investigation is a form of intimacy, and an orgasm is a promise you make to your body that it is still *your* body. She is wearing adrenaline, buzzing with the intoxication of moving how she wants to move: no longer a life model cramping in the centre of a circle. Still combing, I wonder who decides that a house is haunted. Surely the house itself, not the people it invites inside. Squeezed into the tub, we laugh at all the body horror we once treated as a birthright. I continue combing her hair like a metronome or a mother; both timekeepers of some sort. Haunted houses do not frighten those who choreographed the haunting. If you know the schedule of scare tactics, you don't see yourself in the skeletons. Rinsing her hair, I want to ask if pleasure is a haunted house that femininity is invited to enter. I want to ask if she flinched before she felt safe. Instead, I ask her to describe his eyes.

THE FEMME FATALE FORGOES THE PUBLIC BATHROOM

The femme fatale finds me reading on a Friday night. She sighs, leaves the room, and returns with a makeup bag so heavy that it demands both her hands. She perches at my feet and paints my toenails a pink that only exists in cartoon sunsets. She applies shiny, slimy crescents underneath my eyes. She plucks hairs I didn't know I had grown. She grabs my phone and swipes right, one hundred times. I tell her it's very hard to read in these conditions. She laughs and asks how a book can possibly warm a bed. I tell her I am tired of stories where I am the flammable material. She swallows. I tell her I am done being a damsel for desire. She zips up the bag. I tell her that I'm reading a book where the women say more than *save me* or *fuck me*. She crosses her legs, rests her head on the side of my armchair and whispers, *tell me what that sounds like.* Reading to her, I envision this same evening spent elsewhere; clumsy and clutching the sink in a public bathroom, a glass of ice watching from the basin / a woman entering, squealing *I LOVE YOUR MESH* / she would pee with the door open and divulge a dramatic text drafted to her ex / I'd nod, *mmmmm* and look away when she wiped. Women have a habit of making confession booths out of bathroom stalls: somewhere to be lonely aloud.

THE FEMME FATALE SPREADS HER WINGS BUT THEY'RE CROOKED

I come home and catch the femme fatale tracing a wing where her eyelid once was. With a mirror balancing on her lap, she sits cross legged staring at creases. She keeps sighing and starting over, each time spitting on her finger and wiping away wet ink, leaving a patch without foundation. I have never understood the precision of women who can trace new edges onto their eyes with ease. I wonder what it must be like, to define yourself so easily, that you can stay steady even in a passenger seat. As a teenager, I emerged from the bathroom before gigs and closed my eyes in front of my father, asking *are they straight?* My mother always said *yes* too quickly. But the men in my life have mostly looked at me with a closeness I chose to interpret as respect. I wonder what trope the femme fatale would prefer I lean towards today. Am I a protector, or a protractor stroking her cheek? She shushes my footsteps for the ripples they make from the space that surrounds her. I kneel in front of her and instruct *close your eyes*, knowing that I am nobody's beautician, but it's easier to appreciate the brushstrokes of an apparatus you weren't permitted to hold.

THE FEMME FATALE CHAPERONES MY TINDER DATE

Walking to meet a date I've only seen second-hand, I feel the pavement collide with my feet like an agreement that I can run home if I have to. My outfit covers just enough that I will be considered *saveable* if I appear on the news later. Still, I don't ever want to be a candlelit headshot bookmarking a Bible verse. As I walk, the men who pass are made of beer barrels. I hear the femme fatale's voice like a song. She says, *you are not a housewife without a home* and my spine grows extra ligaments. She says, *you are not a mannequin of motherhood* and my hips start to sway the street out of my way. She says, *there is nothing more dangerous than a femme who can both fuck and find herself without a man's direction* and my blood warms like mulled wine. The street opens its legs for me. Crowds part and I am the pink inside. I don't walk, I penetrate. I pass the club where women get roofied, and every pint glass shatters. The traffic light gifts me a bouquet of green figures and I share a grin with everyone wearing lipstick. Still playing like a song stuck in my head, the femme fatale says, *the only way to feel safe on this street is to feel dangerous everywhere else.* So I dig my lilac almonds into my palm. I vow volatility. I bite my bottom lip until it bleeds. Before locating my date, I put both elbows on the bar and am served straightaway. While the wine pours, I tuck a curl behind my ear and realise I am only wearing one earring. The pearl fits between my fingers like a promise.

THE FEMME FATALE TEACHES ME HOW TO TAKE A NUDE

Baby, push your hip to one side and stroke your ribcage as if there is hunger fuelling your hands. This isn't about beautiful ghosts. You need to remain real enough to copy-paste into a fantasy. Men like him own a toolbox for a reason. Suspend your breath like disbelief. Sculpt an optical illusion, exaggerate your edges and crop the ways you just made yourself uncomfortable: the cramped thoracic, the tipped toe, the flexed forearm positioning the phone. Angle yourself as inversion. Proportions are always about the parts of ourselves that we make smaller on purpose. If you play with your nipples he'll assume they're hard in hopes of him. No. Don't smile like that. Unzip your lips. Make sure the bruises from last week's dry-needling could be mistaken for half-healed hickeys. Don't play a damsel in undress. If he wanted to be in a rom-com he would've wrapped his dick in red ribbon before he sent you a picture. If you can convince a butterfly to settle on your hip bone it will emphasise your sharpness without making you appear severe. Don't include your face, never let the recipient catch your expression as you focus on forming into a specific version of yourself. I'm not saying your face is the only site that still belongs to you. But if you show them how your eyes look when you gaze at the reflection of someone you love, they'll know you're lying when you look at them.

I AM NERVOUS ABOUT SLEEPING WITH SOMEONE NEW

So the femme fatale tells me about the time she vomited during a blow job, then swallowed it back up with such enthusiasm that nobody noticed. Tells me that we spend all day filling ourselves with other people's pain, so why not swallow some pleasure for a change. Tells me that the best thing about sex is the moment you forget who you're having it with. How even in love, there is an anonymity that comes when you do. It is a route home. She says that men are so scared of her that they do not long to learn her textures. Says I should be grateful for the ability to stay tameable inside a stranger's stare. When I ask why she doesn't take a break from the aesthetics of alienation, perhaps wear some gingham, she says that she'd lose half of herself if she stopped looking so fatal. Says severity is a chokehold she applies to her own throat. She comes across so harsh that she cannot be holy. Or held. Especially by candlelight. Most men don't write sonnets about women who know what they want.

THE FEMME FATALE UNZIPS THEIR GENDER

Have you ever painted your nails and felt handsome afterwards? She enters the room like a storm ready to become a sky again. *Have you ever been called 'sir' at the supermarket and felt your shoulders swell? Not quite pride, but close, a relative.* The floor is a souvenir of the woman she was today. *Have you ever felt like a drag queen who can't find the un-dressing room?* Her eyelashes are spiders with no webs. Her shoes are heels with no feet. Her hands are full of blood, even when freshly washed. *What is the word for an armour that makes you unsafe in public but is still safer than what you wear in private?* Sometimes we look at each other like men who have just learnt new ways to be affectionate outside the football oval. Or like housewives who just left their high school sweethearts to pursue freelance floristry. *Have you ever painted on a face only to sob it off? Commandeered your contours; no longer bone structure or birthright, but brushstrokes applied so many times they turned tender, like a bruise you hoped would never heal.*

I ASK THE FEMME FATALE WHAT SHE'D LIKE ME TO CALL HER

And expect her to announce something sensual like Ava. Or something ordinary like Sally. Perhaps she's always dreamed of being a Rosie, the kind of woman an admirer will plant then pillage a garden for. I include my own mouth in the question, knowing that each name we choose is also a room we want to enter. She replies, *if I am to be fatal, I don't know who is in danger. Is it the men who flinch? Or is it the person I wake up with when I'm sleeping alone? If there is a volatility in me, let it be mine to define. Call me menace. Like the crowds of lesbians who stood up wearing lavender shirts in the hallways of history. Name me after a purple protest. I want to be a lipstick shade that is smudged after shouting. Call me menace. Of course, men will try to make their way inside everything warm. But the menace manoeuvres her danger, while the fatale brandishes it like a burden. Call me menace. I'll keep the femme. Femme Menace. Call me what your mother's maiden name would be if her mother had been allowed to study at universities. Call me the first phone number you texted a risky 'x' to. Call me the woman who walks into a room and holds the barmaid's breath between her hip bones. Darling, the femme fatale is reserved for the men who want me to stay inside glass. I'm a Femme Menace now.*

THE FEMME MENACE FINDS ME IN THE DRIVEWAY

Curled up crying in the back seat of my own parked car. The tender liminality of being so close to home that you avoid arrival. She knocks on the window like rain. Coaxes me away from my melodrama. I have not sobbed like this since my mother's lap. My chest splitting so painfully I swear all the romance novels were literal. I'm furious with myself, that I couldn't be content with medium-rare love. I wanted well-done and now my plate is empty. Someone else is eating. I wail all the way to the shower. Clutch my waist underwater, my hands like sticky tape. I emerge and apply a band shirt like aloe vera. Dusk erupts into a blue sheen. My bedroom role-plays as an aquarium. I play the song about needing love so badly it morphs your desire into hunger. My palms press into the duvet. My hips dip in the mirror. I re-enact. Hold my own wrist above my head. I perform the leading lady she taught me I could be. I come home to myself. I re-enter the room of my pleasure. I fuck the ghosts of all the women I was meant to become. I burn my knees on the tarmac of masculinity. I shed skins but keep my stretch marks. Once, I defined a good night by how many mouths resuscitated my sense of self. Femme Menace feels sexy before they even reach the bar stool. Femme Menace kisses their own shoulder goodnight. I brush my teeth and the lipstick I leave on the toothbrush stem stains like a lovebite. The Femme Menace still craves the sticky stares of strangers but knows how to pose like a compact mirror, on nights when the gaze grazes our cheek instead of stroking it.

FEMME MENACE AS GUARDIAN

Give me the gift of a grotesque guardian angel. If purity is a priority of my protective onlooker, they'll surely shudder so often that their eyes stay shut. The Femme Menace follows me. I wear thoughts of her like a crossbody clutch: a bag that's barely practical but can hold a lipstick and enough money for any emergency that looks like an unwanted hand. I enter the weekend café and touch this invisible clutch when a booth of teen masculinities turn to assess my fuckability. I stop smiling on the street, start snarling instead. I scream in my car. I light a cigarette in the backyard without asking permission from the air. I spread my legs like real butter on toast. Sometimes I feel the Femme Menace stuck between my teeth. Sometimes I am seducing a stranger and I know her eyes have glossed over mine like contact lenses. Sometimes when a passing car yells, *HEY BABY WHERE ARE YOU GOING* I feel the Femme Menace's fury fill me like boiling water, the kind of rage that makes men scared what you might do. Yet still, the same liquid that brews tea for the people who love me. She says, *it may seem easier to stay angry / but that will split you open / will turn your tenderness into an emergency.* Femme teaches me how to be a menace to everyone other than myself. What good is a guardian angel if they are always gazing coyly away and clasping their hands in prayer? Give me a guardian in black boots and fishnet stockings, someone well equipped to meet me in the mosh pit.

PART THREE

'Born right body / wrong day . . . Tonight, she has dressed / as the inside of a mouth.'

—Joelle Taylor

I AM NOT A WOMAN BUT I STILL CRAVE FEMALE FRIENDSHIP

This city is not a seamstress. We are crumpled in the back seat, both looking too hot to be heading home alone. Your new silk blouse is an architecture that defies buildings, makes skyscrapers self-conscious. My turtleneck frames a face flushed with wine, an adolescence I am both outgrowing and understanding for the first time. Here, we are in some sort of love. It is not the kind of love that makes me long to learn the locations of all your birthmarks, but I can imagine us meeting in a public bathroom a decade from now, comparing lipstick stains and the ways our outlines have eased with age. I can imagine your first sewing machine, which you describe precisely, and how that fabric feels as it is pulled across your lap. I can imagine a book annotated with both our handwriting. Female friendship replaced by femme-ship. Rather than romance sewn across our two bodies, it is a croquette you pass me in the middle of the party, saying something about the ratio of ricotta. It is a power suit of loungewear. It is an unspoken allegiance at the pub. Femme-ship feels nothing like sleepovers in films: it is the way my pronouns grit their teeth inside your mouth when the bartender calls us *ladies.*

TRANS MOSH

My friend tells the gig photographer that Facebook has just started flagging her nipples as female. The vocalist is screaming the word *vulnerable* repeatedly. Their tattoos wink at mine like a private joke. Trans fans put the *grrr* in Riot Grrrl. The guitarist has a string of fairy lights hanging from his backside like a tail, and if he tried to walk home alone we would all become astrologers of dangling ass-stars, and make sure he got safely inside. My limbs sprout new hairs just to give the goosebumps something to latch onto. The vocalist still screaming, *vulnerable vulnerable vulnerable.* The band: shirtless. The crowd: a mirror. I want to rub the sweat of everyone I love into my skin like cocoa butter. Man standing behind me asks why I haven't taken my shirt off too and instead of shrinking I bite back so quick his masculinity tears between my teeth. It looks kinda nice there. Kinda pretty. Kinda femme. His appetite drips onto my Doc Martens where I stomp it out like ash. Glory be to the barricade of bodies like mine. Glory be to the punk music that stopped being about male egos wearing matching hoodies, and started being about the permission that lives inside my throat. Glory be to the prayer that sounds like a growl. Glory be to the congregation of the mosh pit. Baptise me in spit that screams the same manifestos. If you kneel close enough to the altar of a stage, you can see it was never a holy place, but a place where you were allowed to feel holy.

PRETTY SICK

Been watching women in romantic comedies
toss tiny handbags over their shoulders, laugh
without smudging their gloss. They suck lollipops
noiselessly, as if silence is true seduction.

Sometimes, disclosing my illness feels like
coming out (again). I look too young
to be this tenderised. My birthmark
not yet faded. My freckles unironic.

I believe that a body in pain
is a body in the opposite of freefall.

In the film *Second Act*, the protagonist pretends
herself someone else. Not to acquire attention,
but to be successful in ways that can be recognised
by strangers in train carriages.

Last week I answered a work call while wearing a surgical gown,
my underwear bloodying a plastic bag. Mimicking filmic femininity,
I recited a dialogue of betterment; poured wellness down the plastic
pores of the phone, as if my womb could simply unscar itself.

On dance floors where nobody knows, it is easier to convince
myself that my hip clicks like a metronome, not a clock.
This chronic body is a betrayal I am trying to warm towards,
an apartment with damp walls that I stay homesick for.

When I fall in a ballgown
does it soften the impact
or just soften the sound?

A student exclaims, *you look like a main character today*
when I enter the room, red-lipsticked. A louder mouth
collaged over my own. Despite fake pockets, aesthetic
signifiers of fertility still receive more speaking roles.

If I were a romantic lead, my pain would be a plot point:
deserving of dialogue, yet damsel defining.
I don't long for arched redemption.
Let *sick* stay ordinary.
An inconvenience carried in my cutest clutch.
Something tactile that can be folded into squares,
like my grandfather's handkerchief.

If my body falls from a roof tomorrow
it will still be a body in pain, only
falling.

When I confess the chronic of my illness, new lovers reply
to a wounded animal. The signature scent that makes me feel
sexiest contains musk, an ingredient derived from hunted deer.
Each time I prioritise desire, there are consequences. An evening
spent swaying makes my joints protest the morning / I sip pale
ale and each vertebra flinches / I make love and

make pain, simultaneously. I perch on the priority seat
of public transport, wearing stares. They say,
a priority body
couldn't possibly
paint itself pretty.
To be believed, we must be so sick that mirrors forget

to include us. Otherwise, we are merely actors playing
faulty protagonists, who forgot to get better
before the film's final kiss.

Longing, Three Ways

LONGING: HALSEY

You, clothed in shades of salmon so enticing,
they could give a vegetarian an appetite for
something still alive enough to vibrate in the light.
You, twirling your microphone with the confidence
of a man, and the glamorous risk of a teenage
girl. You, who bleed in the wrong direction, just like
I do. You, singing to a sold-out room,
is there somewhere, is there somewhere?
You, the equinox of longing. When I learnt
you were full of futures you once grieved
I clutched my own womb, which has
betrayed me in so many fairy tales,
yet still sheds, like feathers on a dance floor
like dead skin from a sweaty palm, gripping
too tight. That night, when you reached into
the crowd, our hands held a private conversation.
Meanwhile, a stadium of mouths opened
wide like wet, pink phone screens.

As a mosh grabbed for your attention, you held

on. Stroked my palm like a secret message,

laughed kindly into my eyes while I sobbed

and marvelled at my own melodrama.

Thought I had outgrown

these shades of longing.

Is there somewhere?

Is there somewhere?

LONGING: EVERY TIME I BUY FRUIT IT TURNS ROTTEN, FORGOTTEN IN THE BOWL

There was a tattoo between your shoulder blades that I wanted
to press my face against, the way older women check
mangos for ripeness before adding them to baskets.
Thought I was straight until I saw you on a staircase.
Suddenly, I was a hormonal boy fidgeting in his ill-fitting
suit jacket and you were a slow-motion announcement
that clichés can still be beautiful. Let the butterflies enter
the stomach. Let the sunrise arrive, again. My jaw:
a predictable apple, falling into your palm. I wanted
to tangle my ambition around your schedule and argue
about soaking dishes instead of scrubbing them. Often,
my infatuation looks like a strange willingness to wear
an apron. To enact the domesticity I have spent my youth
resisting. Yes, I will build you a treehouse. Yes, I will
bake you a roast dinner basted in honey. Yes, I will scrub
a floor and darn a sock. Yes, I will assure you
that your shoulders make sense. Yes, I will learn to be the man
and the woman you deserve. The last time I saw you, we
held hands in a bar where even the vodka bottles paused
mid-pour. Years later, your chat bubble calls me
baby. Still, we will never share a kitchen counter.

LONGING: DESIRE'S FIRST STEPS

My ligaments have forgotten their first times. Like wooden
chairs stacked outside a church, sacred and left
to rot. Like a graffitied version of a painting that already
exists. Like squatting for a piss while wearing your mother's
wedding dress. The school oval where I probably kiss-chasey'd
my mouth into a memory, now a concrete classroom.
Even the story has been renovated. Like finding your baptism
outfit in an op-shop, but now it fits like a lace garter,
hemline the width of your thigh. Like watching a shirtless driver
reverse-parking during a rainstorm. Like becoming so familiar
with familiarity that you touch it without even trying. Like
dangling your sneakers off a faceless cliff. Your hand catches
mine with the certainty of a trampoline surrounded by netting.
How the first boy who sweated into my palm was not my first
love, but a tech rehearsal. All the stage lights were on, but I was
posing on their perimeter. Lover, I did not look for an
awning. I assumed the church chairs would rot before
they bore the weight of tomorrow's prayers.
Lover, I am standing in my best light
when you reach to me.

RETIRED FROM SLUTDOM, NEW CAREER IN GINGHAM

After Mitski

Responsible heels are just sandals who want to be noticed. Being in love sucks the slut out of me. Monogamy makes masturbating feel like betrayal, not the act itself, but the scenarios my longing constructs. I could tell you the colour of the armchair in the corner. I could give you their phone number. In public bathrooms I smile too much at women in crop tops. Watch their lip gloss relocate their lips. They compliment my gingham ankle dress but they don't spray me with Britney's Fantasy. I miss eyes brushing my midriff like a breeze. I'm not saying I want to get fucked in a garage at the edge of a party—but I'd like to leave the house with that possibility tucked into my bra.

MULTIPLE CHOICE

A.

My gender is a clown suit. Mostly it makes people smile but sometimes it makes people extremely uncomfortable. Sometimes I paint on the face my mother wore before she met my father. More often, I paint the face my father wore the first afternoon he loved my mother. My gender started writing jokes so it could stop being the joke. My gender turns up late to the child's birthday booking. My gender releases the balloons by accident. My gender watches them float away, knowing this is the gentlest introduction to grief. My gender departs on a tiny bicycle. My gender sends an invoice.

B.

My gender is an outfit that Christina Aguilera wears in the 2010 film *Burlesque.* My gender feels sexy in tassels. My gender answers to no body. My gender grew up a country gal then became a big-city-cabaret-star with a hot bartender boyfriend. My gender is envious of Cher. Or, my gender is envious of women who age towards their womanhood, instead of away from it. My gender searches *does Cher have children?* My gender hates being called *a career woman.* My gender wants to make *mum* a non-gendered term. My gender rehearses lines. My gender rehearses androgyny. My gender straddles a piano stool and glances over their shoulder towards an audience of actors. My gender is waiting for Cher to appear behind them in the mirror and apply liner so precise it resembles a tightrope. My gender can belt a chorus after years of silence.

C.

My gender works at a nail salon owned by ghosts. My gender asks what colour you desire today, but all the bottles are named after people you met in the hallways of house parties. My gender files your fingertips into daggers. My gender moisturises your hands like a lover. My gender wants you to feel good about feeling good. My gender is a place where others learn their softness. My gender wonders if you would like two coats of glitter.

D.

My gender sings their own lyrics at karaoke.

E.

My gender is none of the above.

THE DESIRES I'VE RETIRED

I want to be loved like a rom-com protagonist before the closing credits, yet sustain a sex life that I'm scared my neighbours will overhear. Want to come home from my wholesome date and forget where the light switch is located. Want to have the kind of orgasm that clears your mind like a whiteboard wiped at the end of a lesson. Want to retrieve my own synaesthesia, which embodies orgasms as orange swatches, after months of greyscale pleasure. Desire walked out of my relationship like a husband already making new promises. Sometimes he visits to collect his belongings, but he is always leaving, even in the moment he arrives. I want to experience longing like two skyscrapers who touch the same clouds, moments apart. Want to role-play a high risk body double balanced on a string between them, rope stretched like saliva mid-snog. I want to be the woman I was wearing before I contracted monogamy. Sometimes when I touch myself, I remember a drunk first date I had years ago, when a new man reached for my hand; the lightning I wanted to be struck by.

ETYMOLOGY OF A WARM PLACE

A vulgarity that longs to be softened and spoken with love. I sleep with a cross-stitched vision of you hanging over my bedframe. The first time, my mother paused the movie to spit a warning, *you must never, never use that word*. What does it mean for the worst word in her world to have its hometown inside of me? Every pap smear scrapes and samples the word. Every lover's tongue tries to excavate the word. Every time I flood, the word emerges clearly, like engraved pavement after rain. I once used a lace garter to tourniquet my shame. My friends called me the word and it meant a warm place. Wallets opened to view my word, like freshly painted artwork. *Vagina* comes from the Latin for sheath, but it has been a lifetime since I tried to tessellate sharp things inside of myself and called this love. Call me *kott*. Call me *kunta*. Call me *cunēre*. Teach me to own the origin story my mother was afraid of. Cunt is a curse word that pays its own tuition, just to be allowed into love's mouth. A balancing between *baby* and breath. A cross-stitch above my bed, which shows no signs of the needle that once defined it.

PORTRAIT OF THE QUEER BODY AS DIFFICULT LACE

//

A utopia where I am lace choreographed to look like rope,
                    instead of rope choreographed to look like lace.
Something masculine made of feminine materials /
        something feminine made of masculine materials.
A skyscraper with leadlight windows is not necessarily a church.
  A forest cabin full of fax machines daydreams of business meetings.
What I mean is, the materials that make us do not form metaphors,
until they are woven together, and placed in front of audiences
who are hungry   to meet themselves   in untouchable rooms.

//

I want to stick my fingers through you like a ripe
afternoon. The gaps between your teeth
are songs without lyrics. Is my desire simply
a relocation of mirrors into inconvenient
corridors? Desperate to collage
over my reflection, I will contort
myself into craft materials. Gazing at figures
who gaze away from the peacocks
which rest their beautiful, heavy heads
upon manhood's open palm.

//

Onlookers often presume the politeness of lace.
Disregard its disobedience, how absence gossips
with light: an architecture of insinuation.
My body brushes the weaver's hand as I sit behind the tapestry.
                    His attention turns my tattoos into tiny collaborations.

//

What is masculinity   if not a bunch   of small needles
   that could complete   something beautiful   if they were held
for a little longer?   What is my   bare torso
      if not an architecture   of shadows   allowed on display
only during   specific hours?

//

Of course, I am sitting in front of a shirtless man, writing about his absent hands.

//

In an adjacent room, women perform a procession of armoured selves. But I am busy choking on my misplaced boyhood, like a sob in public space. A faucet I did not know was loose until the sink started kissing the kitchen floor.

//

The staff member behind the front desk asks if you'd like to spray yourself with the same scent that baptises the bottom of the bobbin lace each morning. She'll suggest you spray it again on a square of cardboard: regeneration slides into your pocket. Your private heavens are a scent that strangers notice but cannot identify. You, who desire dramatic invisibility. You, who have posed on the windowsills of dark rooms where strangers peered in and said they saw nothing. What is a queer body if not a memory that nobody else can see, even if you describe it in detail? Here, rope suspends disbelief, becomes difficult lace which, like longing, is both unfinished and unfinishable. A scent dissipating in the moment it is sprayed.

//

Fouché describes this weaving technique as *near inhuman craftsmanship* and I consider the queer body as beyond human,   as tender monstrosity;   a fantasy that fantasises about itself. When I desire the man with a peacock in his hand, I am foraging for myself in him. If any part of me is related to rebirth, let me be the family member who disrupts a dinner table: the cousin drowning aloud. What is queerness, if not rope playing dress-ups with lace? What is an inherited utopia, if not a shadow that reimagines my skin as stained glass?

BALANCING ACT

There is a tightrope in my kitchen that nobody else can see. Made from thread that shines like spider web. Yet even when I clamber, claw at cupboards, beg to break the lineage, it will not untether itself. My love, much taller than me, bangs their head on the thread and it does not constrict around their brain. Their bowl stays the same size. Not ocean, not lake, just a ceramic circumference that hasn't changed since yesterday. I walk for hours at my favourite park, the footpath like an infinity loop on Tumblr's teenage wrist. There is no achievement in repeating the same routine until the ache relocates from your mind to your hips, but there is sustenance in repetition. Once, controlling my illness meant controlling my mouth. Now I know that even streetlights feel hunger. I do not mention the tightrope to my mother. Still, she flinches when she opens the fridge and silver thread shudders above. My father delivers Tupperware containers stocked with soft landings. My recovering body a balancing act. Starvation is an imaginary friend I am grieving. My smallness; a sequence of stick figures engraved on splashback tiles. Before bed, I lie on the kitchen floor staring upwards. Tangled like an infinity loop, the tightrope stares back: a shard of mirror stretched too thin to see myself in.

CRYSTALLINE

The afternoon an engagement ring appeared on your finger, you wouldn't answer any of my questions. It was as if I was passing the billboard too fast to read what was written on the sign. Still, I saw it. You always laugh at my jokes. Once we spent twenty minutes discussing the arrangement of your office. You'd swapped our chairs and my brain couldn't handle the disruption. You made it a metaphor, I made it a punchline. Once you met my dad in person after meeting him in all my stories. In the waiting room we sat on different sides of each other than we did in front of you. I never mentioned what he looked like, so I don't know if you expected his eyes to be kind like mine. Your hair is long and impossibly blonde like an anaemic waterfall during the bright conception of the earth. You cross your legs like a model on a television show. You always look like a rich woman who has purchased an outfit specifically for the resort poolside, or a rich woman heading to meet her most recent ex-husband's lawyer. Last year when I asked how you maintain emotional distance while talking to awful people, you replied that you refuse to treat anyone you can't empathise with, and I wished for a future where I could afford that. Sometimes you laugh too much during our sessions and I watch you trying to hold in all your separate selves. You know that my humour is an outfit I chose for this room. There is an alternate universe where we are two women in expensive silk wrap skirts with damp hems, on our way to the pool, and I'm still deciding if I want to drown in the bartender or just drown.

THE WOMEN OF THE BEAT MUSEUM ARE DISPLAYED IN A SEPARATE CABINET

Being a young femme who travels alone is like being the narrator of a true crime podcast. I premeditated every murder, prepared my throat to scream in a pretty pitch of panic. Stark Doc Martens, gifted for this trip, met the carpet of The Beat Museum. After inspecting Ginsberg's desk and pondering the permanence of men, your woodworked voice asked about Australian poetry. I asked after Ruth and Diane. You asked if I wanted to get a drink. Like those women in glass cabinets, I could've been convinced to write adjacent rooms for your genius. How smitten I was with my fist unclenching in your coat pocket. When I arrived in San Francisco I wanted an alleyway named after me. At the airport, I proclaimed that you were the first person I had loved without using a pseudonym.

I lied: I don't remember the carpet, but the narrator inside of me says it would've caught the bloodstains best.

UGLIEST GIRL AT THE PARTY

'Recently a student of mine said for her the prose poem *is like the ugliest girl at the party who is having the best time.* To which I say, *Party on.*'

—Beckian Fritz Goldberg

If you're telling me the prose poem has lipstick on her teeth, it means you were already looking at her mouth. If corsets are considered glamorous, then why not this constraint? You can tie this poem to your bedposts, stretch her edges until they gasp, and still she will be a prose poem. I know some skinny poems are asked to smile more. I know width is not always welcome. I know a page is just another alleyway that the poem is trying to survive. But this poem is heading to the party anyway, ignoring the instructions of her French fathers. Her dress: a slow reveal threatening to spill, hemline grasping the cusp of a cheek crease. This poem seduces men for free drinks then stares at her phone while they brag about owning images. This poem would rather be looked at than looked after. There is an elastic end to her evening. This poem moves her edges side to side without breaking breath, an engine humming inside, her limbs tumbling like unbroken lines. Besides, even the least beautiful girl at the party is still beautiful.

WAITING FOR YOU TO TEXT BACK

I would cut out my bladder and hold it in my hands. I would ascend a building just to tell you about the dusty tops of streetlights. I would introduce myself to strangers. I would ingest your name like a password. I would wear a locket guarding your childhood pet's ashes. I would meet your mistress and find a polite way to be jealous. I would take singing lessons so I could accompany the freeway's radio. I would donate all my everyday underwear then negotiate with the tiny buttons of your business shirts. I would microwave every fantasy of us, ready to eat, to be eaten. I am a wolf without teeth at your doorstep. I am a burning hotel room with a beautiful bathtub. I would become the postbox and open my mouth in a perfect circle, waiting for you to measure, then tell me you want me wider.

EKPHRASIS: DICK PIC

Every day of the year is the anniversary of someone, somewhere, falling in love. Today is a day I open a dick pic while walking in the rain. The dick looks like a wide sunrise. I have worn so many new socks since I stopped sleeping well beside you. I have worn so many new selves, have put them between my teeth without biting down. I am spitting on a man instead of calling him a house key. I am choking on the opposite of forever. When asking for what I want, I come closer to enacting manhood. I state my desire as if stating the time of day after looking at my wrist. The last time I had sex with someone I loved, I imagined another man returning from football training covered in dirt, with spiky soles, his urgency grabbing me like a mark he was hungry to make. I imagined soil and what it would feel like to collaborate so overtly, to advertise someone's surname on my back. I fell out of love the same way a dick pic arrives in the rain, a stumbling shock that settles into a daily routine. Now I am curating a glass cabinet of masculinities: not mirrors, but case studies. If I ever get a tattoo above my eyebrow, it will read *tender.*

DESIRE

Do I deserve a linen cupboard? What would I fold?

UNMADE

A tour guide gestures to a four-poster bed, which was dismantled
into sections for boat transportation, the same way we must split
ourselves into simplified mouthfuls, in order to be
remembered—

Off-white linen is displayed unmade, yet posed precisely
(as if slumber had only just departed) beyond a rose
coloured rope that prevents eyes from becoming hands,
stops dust turning sticky with curiosity.

This public memory; curated then tousled by professionals
who own refrigerators and washing machines,
who flush toilets during the night and complain
about the temperature of bathwater while they
scroll and screenshot photographs of the past.

I want to know what side she slept on. If bedpans
were billboards that clarified the realities of the body.
Handwashed shame stains differently, like a knotted
rag that refuses to release what it knows.

In another suburb, the brass bed I was conceived
upon remains pressed against a wall of my childhood
home. My current frame makes a mockery of heritage,
wearing a costume of wood, creaking a warning.

Neither of these are unmade in the mouths of
tour guides. My pillowcase is not a national treasure.
But perhaps if I erected a story with enough absence
the significance would emerge slowly, like a stretch mark
that shows where the body came from, even
after the body has arrived.

I am told that a committee of experts argued about the disrespect
of displaying an unmade marriage bed. Said a woman like *her*
would never do that. Would never rest on imperfection—
as if hospital corners define a lineage, or an inheritance,
or a good reason to be remembered.

Let it be known that I always slept on the side
nearest to the wall. To the left of my lover, heavy on
my stomach, breasts flattened against morning's breath.

Let the tour guide announce,
some months sadness unmade her.
Still, she rested upon what remained.
She demanded to be remembered not only
for her grief, but never without it.

WHEN DOES YOUR BODY FEEL LIKE IT BELONGS TO YOU?

Queer bodies dance in ordinary ways.
Reaching for tea. Rushing for hands.
My loves: when I am dancing alone
I am dancing beside you. We arrive
like daylight. Spin in wide circles
with wide joy. We are a film
that will never be made; all this glory
too gory, all this hunger too porous.
Monologues slip
                                        through our ungritted teeth.

MALE FANTASY

Catcalled at Coles, again. Frozen aisle fantasies. Day one blood dripping, threatening to show itself to the shopping centre. The man's mouth doesn't perceive a body, only what he could do with it. Grotesque beneath my garment. I imagine sticking my fist beneath the waistband, scooping a clot, smearing it on my cheeks. Not like war paint, like blush. A proclamation that makes me feel pretty, even though it signifies fertility. In the nineteenth century when blush was banished, a public sin associated with promiscuity, women still stood in the corners of rooms pinching their cheeks before meeting suitors. I imagine this covert choreography of desire, as he follows me to the *Feminine Hygiene* aisle. Each moment I move closer to producing a paddle pool of unspeakable pink. Not feminine, but yes hygienic. Good for gardens. A fruitful fertiliser. I want to make that catcaller didactic. I want to pour a can of diced beetroot into his tote bag. I want to coat his car bonnet with potent period poop. I want to shriek until the supermarket smoke detectors notice the burning inside my throat. But today, I need all that energy just to get myself back to bed. The man inspects a cut of raw meat and doesn't perceive an animal, something that once bled: only the satisfaction he surely deserves to devour. Before blush was sold in supermarkets, some used strawberry juice instead. Between my legs, a sticky reminder of the small ways we sweeten our survival.

ODE TO MY KNEECAPS

You who contribute to holding me
up, but never take the credit.
You silent sermon in the collapsing
cathedral hall of my body.
You lyrics after the chorus, living
forgotten in the liquid centre of noise.

You tougher, larger, rounder knuckles.
You grazed excuse for an epiphany.
You always prepared for impact.
You who have never been complimented.
You shield sewn into my nonchalance.
You good ending to a bad story.

Ode to my kneecaps, who I always slice during shaving.
You the canvas of my clumsiness. You who click
your invisible tongue at cold weather.

Oh kneecaps, you equator of ankle
and thigh. You who feel the breeze
through torn windows
of my dungarees.

Oh kneecaps, you insistent creases.
You section of wandering skull.
You who have never been itchy.
You unsubtle bone, not bothering to hide.

Oh kneecaps!
You twin peaks. You rock-hard
boob shapes. You carpet burn
after coitus. You altar of romance.
You who have never been too big
or too small
for an outfit.
You cement poured in by my parents.
You faulty GPS I was born with. You flag
who has only ever felt half-mast.

Ode to my kneecaps, the breadwinner of my body.
The bruise-winner of my best dance moves.

There are so many odes to collarbones,
I'm sorry I didn't look lower sooner.
You unassuming barricade,
a mountain I can curl around
on the train ride home.

Dressing: Three Garments

ONE: CORSETRY ON THE WASHING LINE

Remove a corset from the frame and the structure becomes a useless ribcage. Once I thought my waist had to be a convenient circumference. Now I grow into all the garments I was desperate to shed. Beating chests should stay in pop punk lyrics, I want to watch the way a beaten carpet sheds. Our skin is a stain we cannot see on the upholstery. Yet the couch creases are a narrow stomach, easily satiated by socks and my one pair of sexy-on-purpose underwear. All the suits I own were special to someone else first. (Almost) nobody purchases purple velour for a practical occasion. If a baby queer one day walks into an op-shop and gasps at the way lilac lets their reflection be their reflection, will I ever be entirely gone? I don't want to be immortal like a Cullen, but I'd like to supervise what souvenirs the corset of my life leaves upon the skin of my death. I'm not scared of death but I am terrified of white nightgowns. If obedient womanhood is required for remembrance, gift me an absent eulogy. What is a corset beyond the body, if not an architecture of memory? After the house is abandoned, someone will surely try to renovate the broken windows into stained glass, so a building can be mourned as if it were once a church.

TWO: PLEASE, CHOOSE THE 100% COTTON ONES

How will the mortician know which of my underwear is the most comfortable? I don't want to enter eternity with a wedgie. Would it be better to be buried commando, letting my pussy moisten with the decomposing demands of soil? Would worms slither into the afterlife version of my DMs? If I have a heavy period on the day that I die, will the blood stay forever frozen, like a raspberry icy pole? My corpse-crotch stained while someone recites a sonnet beside a bouquet of roses that are not red enough. I'm not trying to be crude. I realise that comfort is for the living. But consider what it might feel like to be haunted by a ghost who has a UTI.

THREE: HAND ME DOWN

I wore Grandad's grey knit jumper the first time I stood in snow. My sweethearts watched me blur between parked cars and scrape sentimentality as if it could stay solid in my grasp. If I breed, I hope my grandchildren will wear my favourite pyjamas to the pride parade. I hope they stain my best dress on a dance floor. I hope they snip the sleeves from my purple suit, sew all the floral prints into protest signs. I hope they wrap my wardrobe around their lovers. I hope they pull on inheritance like a baggy shirt the morning after. If I am allowed to have a legacy, let it be well worn.

LITTLE ONE

Little one, I have thought of you in absolutes.
My tired body becoming your tired body.
A tuning fork beneath my pillow
to decipher the pitch of your desires.

I have barely raised a garden bed. Abandoned
the success story of hospital corners. Betrothed
myself to screens and books. Warmed my
armchair instead of warming my mattress.

Yet I have also been a scholar of the pigeons
who build nests without permission. I taught
a terrified tabby to sleep deeply in my arms.
I have attended so many appointments about you,
although you were barely a breeze that passed

through those rooms. Goosebumped my legs beneath
paper sheets. Urinated into plastic portals that promised
precognition. I have put aside your pocket money—
which is to say, I researched the cost of freezing a future.

My body, heat-mapped like a suburb
you will one day sprint through, without
even noticing what was planted for you.

During the worst Endo bloats, I have prayed
with both palms on my belly. Pretended
in the shower, bathtub, bedroom mirror.
I have played house with this body.
I have played hope with this body.

There is an old photograph of my mother standing outside
my childhood home: angsty perm and thick-rimmed glasses,
a sweater pulled to her sternum. She holds her stomach like
a bundle of blankets she is carrying towards someone she loves.

When the boardroom asks about my ten-year plan,
your small fist fills my mouth like an apricot. An endorheic
basin inside of me dreams of touching an ocean.

Motherhood may arrive differently, but still I will be
a mother. We do not catch the rain and call it seawater.
Little one, my love for you will nurture a garden until Eden
is envious, until pigeons take notes on my nesting,
until all the weeping in waiting rooms
can be rewritten as tiny water births.

WOMANHOOD IS A HUNGRY MIRROR, STRUGGLING TO SWALLOW ITS OWN REFLECTION

We watch ourselves in the eyes of our lovers. Tie our fingers to their temples. Lace our throats around their hands. When I hold his gaze, I become my bedroom mirror / an aluminium bathtub / a camera lens covered in lipstick. Silver coins cascade out my mouth. A shard of glass carves my silhouette onto a stage. A man who doesn't know me says he loves me, and I let him. I am a skilful mirror, womanhood taught me this. I speak to myself inside someone else's stare. My shivers are warm here. My body is an ocean that nobody else dares to swim in. I look at myself and flinch, but refuse to retreat. I look at myself again. I look like myself again.

MY FEAR AND MY FEMME SHARE A SUBURB

Femininity wasn't what made me vulnerable, even though it made me visible / my femininity is not a survival instinct, it is a song.

ENCORE

Femininity made
my survival a song.

AUTHOR NOTES

Gratitude to the stages, publications and organisations that were the first homes for earlier versions of these poems. The writing received support from Express Media's Kat Muscat Fellowship (with special thanks to the Muscat family); the National Trust of Western Australia; *Westerly* magazine's inaugural Mid-Career Fellowship; the Katharine Susannah Prichard Writers' Centre; and Varuna, The National Writers' House, which awarded me the inaugural Pitch Me! Fellowship and the 2022 Varuna Poetry Flagship Fellowship.

Dress Rehearsals was developed from the creative product of my PhD and honours manuscripts, completed at Curtin University under the supervision of Dr Deborah Hunn, Dr Christina Lee and Dr Susan Bradley Smith. Special thanks to executive supervisor Dr Cassandra Atherton, whose flower-power mentorship reignited my love for prose poetry. My PhD was supported by an Australian Government Research Training Program Scholarship.

The book's epigraph is borrowed from 'Woman (In Mirror)' by La Dispute (*Rooms of the House*, 2014).

The three epigraphs that introduce each section are borrowed from Tavi Gevinson, 'The Infinity Diaries' (*Rookie* magazine, 2016); Christina Grübler, '*Basic Instinct* with a twist: How the femmes fatales of *Killing Eve* queer the gendered politics of crime television' (*Gender Forum*, no. 79, 2021); and Joelle Taylor, 'Valentine' (*C+nto and Othered Poems*, Westbourne Press, 2021).

When I Grow Up I Want To Be The Merch Girl was commissioned for Red Room Poetry's National Poetry Month 2021. Thank you to Anne-Marie Te Whiu and David Stavanger.

Impulse previously appeared in *Cordite Poetry Review*, no. 106, 2022.

Uniform was drafted during an online writing group for transgender and gender diverse young people, funded by City of Melbourne Libraries and facilitated by two of the most generous authors and loving friends I know: Alison Evans and Nevo Zisin. Thank you to the members of that group; this book would not exist without my LGBTQIA+ community. The poem begins with a quote from 'Dress' by Mary Jean Chan (*Flèche*, Faber & Faber, 2021). The dictionary definition was borrowed from Lexico online dictionary, powered by Oxford University Press.

Harry Styles Is Interviewed On A Beach And The Horizon Aligns With His Sighs previously appeared in *Going Down Swinging* (October 2020), with editorial feedback from Georgia Coldebella. The poem responds to a YouTube interview between Harry Styles and Zane Lowe ('Harry Styles: "Fine Line" Interview', YouTube, 2019).

I Grew Up A Shadow Girl, With A Man Outlined Inside Me won the 2020 Shadow Catchers Competition, supported by Red Room

Poetry, and was exhibited at the Art Gallery of New South Wales. The poem is an ekphrastic response to the photograph *The Photographer's Shadow* by Olive Cotton (circa 1935).

Sonnet For Longing is informed by 'Sonnet for Heartbreak' by Sam Rush (*Swallow*, Sibling Rivalry Press, 2021) and 'Sonnet' by Terrance Hayes (*Hip Logic*, Penguin, 2002).

Dichotomy was written in consideration of *Fangirls: Scenes from modern music culture* by Hannah Ewens (Quadrille Publishing, 2019).

Child Of The Hurricane won first prize in the 2019 Mundaring Poetry Competition. The title is borrowed from *Child of the Hurricane: An autobiography* by Katharine Susannah Prichard (Angus & Robertson, 1963).

Most People I Know Have Had Sex While Listening To The Arctic Monkeys begins with a quote from 'Little Beast' by Richard Siken (*Crush*, Yale University Press, 2005).

Silence In Three Parts previously appeared in *Rabbit 30: The Long Poem* (2020).

I Misgender Myself In The Memories was written for the event Neon Readings, organised by Joni Boyd and Saoirse Nash. It begins with a quote from 'I Only Misgender Myself When Fleetwood Mac Comes On' by Lyd Havens (*Chokecherry*, Game Over Books, 2021).

Spiders On My Lash Line quotes Boat Show's song 'Staying Alive' (*Groundbreaking Masterpiece*, 2017).

Trans Mosh was drafted during a workshop with Joelle Taylor organised by Red Room Poetry. The poem quotes Dong Fang's song 'Vulnerable' (*Jarrah*, 2022) and previously appeared in *Rabbit 36: The Art Issue* (2022).

Pretty Sick was previously published by *Overland* literary journal. It was shortlisted in *Overland*'s 2021 Judith Wright Poetry Prize and *Australian Book Review*'s 2021 Peter Porter Poetry Prize. The poem is dedicated to Andrew Sutherland.

Longing, Three Ways was written during my 2021 Mid-Career Fellowship with *Westerly* magazine. This sequence appeared in *Westerly 66.1* and received editorial support from Dr Cassandra Atherton, Dr Daniel Juckes, Dr Catherine Noske and Dr Josephine Taylor. 'Is There Somewhere?' is a song by Halsey (*Room 93*, 2015). **Every Time I Buy Fruit It Turns Rotten, Forgotten In The Bowl** was previously published in *Australian Poetry Anthology*, vol. 9 (2021).

Retired From Slutdom, New Career In Gingham references Mitski's album title *Retired from Sad, New Career in Business* (2013).

Multiple Choice previously appeared in *Australian Poetry Anthology*, vol. 12, issue 1 (2022) and *In Flux: Trans* and gender-diverse reflections and imaginings* (Thousand Threads Press, 2022).

Etymology Of A Warm Place was drafted during a 2021 workshop with Sam Rush, organised by Awful Good Writers.

Portrait Of The Queer Body As Difficult Lace is an ekphrastic response to Pierre Fouché's *The Little Binche Peacock and Other Utopian Dreams*, exhibited in the 2021 Indian Ocean Craft Triennial Australia at John Curtin Gallery. The final stanza includes a quote from Fouché's online artist statement. The poem previously appeared in *Meniscus Journal*, vol. 9, issue 2, 2021.

Balancing Act previously appeared in *Admissions: Voices within mental health* (Upswell Press, 2022).

Crystalline was drafted during an online writing session with dear friend Katie McAllister.

The Women Of The Beat Museum Are Displayed In A Separate Cabinet was written in consideration of *Life of the Party* by Olivia Gatwood (Penguin, 2019).

Ugliest Girl At The Party quotes Beckian Fritz Goldberg in 'Crashing the Party: Going home with the prose poem you want' (*The Rose Metal Press Field Guide to Prose Poetry: Contemporary poets in discussion and practice*, Rose Metal Press, 2010).

Unmade was awarded first place in the 2020 Tom Collins Poetry Prize by the Fellowship of Australian Writers, Western Australia. A version was previously published in *Australian Poetry Anthology*, vol. 9, 2021. The poem was written during a writing residency supported by the National Trust of Western Australia.

When Does Your Body Feel Like It Belongs To You? is an excerpt from a longer collaborative piece originally written for the 2021 Emerging Writers' Festival.

Male Fantasy references a song title from *Happier Than Ever* by Billie Eilish (2021).

Ode To My Kneecaps previously appeared in *How to be Held* by Maddie Godfrey (Burning Eye Books, 2018). Thank you to Clive Birnie, Kate Birnie and Bridget Hart.

Dressing: Three Garments is an ekphrastic response to Frances Harvey's fashion collection *Afterlife* (2021).

ACKNOWLEDGEMENTS

Dress Rehearsals was written on Whadjuk Noongar land, with respect and gratitude to the custodianship and storytelling of Indigenous Elders, past and present. The gender binary is a colonial construct, and I pay my respects to LGBTQIA+ First Nations peoples and their expressions of gender. This place always was and always will be Aboriginal land.

This collection documents a decade of performing femininity, hence I cannot possibly name everyone who kept me alive during this time, but utmost gratitude and love to Ross and Sadie, my proudest fangirls.

Thank you to the brilliant, brave and beautiful women who first believed in this book: Grace Heifetz of Left Bank Literary and Nakkiah Lui of Joan Press. Thank you to Fiona Wright for a sharp editorial gaze, Kaya Wilson for their thoughtful reading, Clara Finlay for an impressive attention to detail, and the enthusiastic Allen & Unwin team (including, but not limited to, Genevieve Buzo, Kelly Fagan and Angela Handley).

The first poems I knew were lyrics yelled in mosh pits. Gratitude to La Dispute, the first band I ever loved, who continue to make fandom a place where I feel safe and seen.

We are all rehearsing and performing the ways we wear gender, some of us are simply more aware of this. Thank you to transgender, non-binary and gender-nonconforming friends, lovers, writers and musicians, who provide mirrors in which I have been able to see myself.

The dressing rooms of gender haven't always been a place of joy, but maybe they can be.

ABOUT THE AUTHOR

Madison Godfrey is a writer, editor and educator. They live on Whadjuk Noongar land. Madison has performed poetry at the Sydney Opera House, the Royal Albert Hall, St Paul's Cathedral and Glastonbury Festival. In 2021 they were awarded the Western Australian Youth Award for Creative Contributions. Madison's great loves include the colour purple and a rescue cat named Sylvia.